FIRE LOOKOUT OUTHOUSES

La Vaughn Vanderburg Kemnow

MountAins West
Publishing

~

ISBN: 978-0-9996067-8-0

Photos

Front Cover

      Hickman Butte, Mt. Hood National Forest, Oregon

Back Cover

      Clockwise from upper left: Rancheria Rock, Wheeler County, Oregon; South Baldy, Malheur County, Oregon; Unidentified; Timber Mountain, Colville National Forest, Washington; Paradise Craggy, Siskiyou County, California; Roman Nose, Siuslaw National Forest, Oregon; Monument Mountain, Grant County, Oregon; Sheephorn Mountain, Salmon National Forest, Idaho. Center: Snowboard Ridge, Wheeler County, Oregon

Interior and cover photos by La Vaughn Vanderburg Kemnow, except as noted

Fire Lookout Outhouses

This is a companion book to the thirteen-book series, Fire Lookouts. The Fire Lookouts series subtitles are:

The Early Years

The Middle Years

The Later Years

Of Mules and Men

Where There's Smoke

Hot, Dry, Windy, Wet, Frozen Electrified and Horrified

Life and Limb

Women in High Places

Smoke Signals, Dynamite, Pigeons, Heliographs, Telephones and Radios

Rattlesnakes, Porcupines, Cougars, and Bears

Endings and Oddities

Vandals, Thieves, and Firebugs

Civilian Conservation Corps

Other titles by this author are Alaska Bush Mother (a memoir); and Slavery Among the Indians of the Northwest (a research paper). Also published by this author is a book of hunting stories (nonfiction) by her father Warren Vanderburg.

Lookout Outhouses

The "Necessary House," otherwise known as an outhouse or toilet, is an essential part of the accommodations needed to set up a safe and efficient environment for the people who staff fire lookouts. They must be neither too close to nor too far from the lookout. In some areas, because of lack of space and/or rocky terrain, they are built over the edge of a cliff. While most are of wood construction, some are of stone, concrete, or man-made molded materials.

Black Butte

Malheur National Forest, Grant County, Oregon

Black Butte June 11, 2016

Decorations on the wall
To make it feel like home
It adds a bit of color there
Although it's monochrome

Frazier Point

Whitman National Forest, Malheur National Forest, Oregon

Frazier Point, June 12, 2016

January 3, 1937: "The fire lookout who scans the lonely expanse of pine forest from Frazier Point, between Burns and Prairie City, next summer will do so from the dizzy level of a [one] hundred foot wooden tower, which is the pride of its recent C.C.C. builders. The high tower is in Malheur National Forest...built of treated Douglas fir.

A little cabin in the woods
To serve that big high tower
Where you can sit and think a while
Beside a leafy bower

Antelope Mountain

Malheur National Forest, Grant County, Oregon

Antelope Lookout
6-12-2016

1929: A 20-foot timber tower with an L-4 gable roof cab was constructed. This tower had no catwalk. *(Malheur National Forest Archive Files)*

1974: "Special Project Specifications: General – The project consists of moving an existing 30-foot lookout tower and flattop lookout house structure complete located on Lake Butte in Section 30, T.11Sl, R.32E., to Antelope Mountain...remove and dispose of existing 20-foot lookout tower and house at Antelope Mountain. The Government will plow the snow off the roads to both the Lake Butte and Antelope Mountain sites.

The Government estimates the total weight of the lookout at Lake Butte to be approximately 22,500 pounds, broken down as follows: House-12,000pounds; tower-10,500 pounds...the contractor shall be responsible for moving and disposing of the existing structure at Antelope Mountain." *(Malheur National Forest Archives File)*

Would you invade this packrat haven
If you were in a rush?
How much wiser it might be
To go out in the brush

Monument Peak

Bureau of Land Management, Malheur County, Oregon

Monument Peak 12-30, 2012

August 28, 1958: "Two temporary fire lookouts are watching over a wide area this fire season. One is on Lookout Mountain in the Baker district. The other is on Monument Peak east of Juntura." *(Baker Record-Courier)*

*This toilet's day has come and gone
With no house it looks so bare
But it surely served its tenants well
Those lookouts who were stationed there*

Lookout Rock

Fremont National Forest, Lake County, Oregon

Lookout Rock January 5, 2013

Prior to the erection of the first tower a tree with a crow's nest stood near where the tower is now located.

July 18, 1947: "Kenneth Carlson, who was the forest lookout on Lookout rock last summer is moving to Keno springs guard station." "The Bly ranger district still needs a good man with a car for the Lookout rock position." *(Herald and News)*

1959: From the inspection report made by the Regional Office of Engineering on September 10th: "The lookout tower is an 8-legged sawn timber tower, 20 feet in height. The house is the 14x14 size. Tower and house were constructed by CCC project in 1932. The inspection found the lookout premises and the house living quarters in clean and orderly condition.

1962: From final construction report: "Road ended approximately 500 feet and 1000 feet below the job site. Packing by horses not practical."

1972: Inspection report: "There are four or five places where woodpeckers have been working on the outside. The largest hole is approximately four inches long and three inches wide through the side of the lathing. The facility is in good shape for an unused lookout. The toilet is unsatisfactory, no pit due to rock."

Here the flying camera crashed
And could be used no more
That big rock caused its downfall
So back to the camera store!

Timber Mountain

Colville National Forest, Pend Oreille County, Washington

Timber Mountain September 22, 2012

A tree grew up; the door fell down
But does it really matter?
The tree got cut; the door leaned up
To muffle the pitter-patter

Franson Peak

Department of Natural Resources, Ferry County, Washington

Franson Peak September 21, 2012

This little outhouse looks so neat
Standing stark and clean
You can sit as long as you want
And take in the lovely scene

South Baldy Mountain

Colville national Forest, Washington

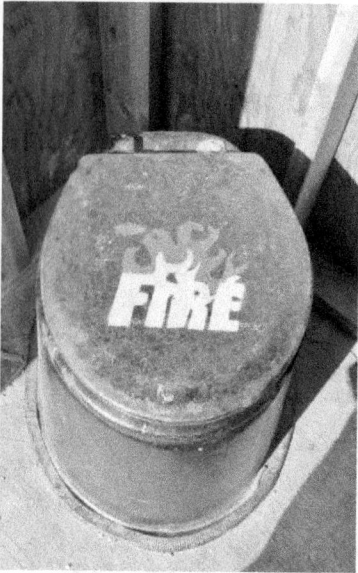

South Baldy 9-24-2012

July 14, 1925: "Paul Blickensdorfer, lookout at South Baldy...was killed by the electrical storm...a student at the University of Idaho. His father is a physician at Cincinnati, O....He was sleeping on the floor of the lookout cabin, having given up his bed to visiting forest officials, when killed. No others in the cabin were injured. *(Morning Oregonian)*

"Fire in the hole" they shout
When a blast is due to happen
So clear the way and dash inside
And don't be caught a'nappin'

Paradise Craggy

California Department of Forestry, Siskiyou County, California

Photo by Ron Kemnow October 12, 2011

Poles were set in February 1932 for the telephone line for the new Paradise Lookout.

This craggy mountain lacks in space
At its very top
A gust of wind can send you off
You'll find it's quite a drop

Big Butte

Umatilla National Forest, Asotin County, Washington

During a wind storm the winter of 2010-11 a tree fell across one of the guy cables causing that tower leg to shear off at one of the higher leg joints.

Big Butte
Washington
August 2011

September 1929: "After three days on the lonesome lookout of Anatone Butte, the lookout man became ill. He was taken to a doctor and returned to the job ten days later. One day on the lookout he became ill again and had to be replaced. There were reports to the effect that the illness was caused by goblins who came in the nighttime and made frightful noises about the weird and lonesome lookout station." *(Six Twenty-Six)*

The tower had a broken leg
A tree had caused the rent
But the little outhouse was unharmed
And it was heaven sent

Baker Point

Sequoia National Forest, Tulare County, California

In 1941 a new lookout on Baker Ridge was planned to take the place of the one on Sunday Ridge.

Baker Point 2011

July 14, 1959: "A crackling brush fire which has consumed 5,000 acres in Sequoia National Park since lightning set it Saturday roared into tall timber despite the efforts of 500 firefighters and 200 Zuni Indian experts. It forced the evacuation of 2,000 summer resort guests ...and seriously burned two firefighters...burning west to Baker Ridge where a woman lookout was evacuated." *(The Times)*

Another drop, a long way down
If you should miss the trail
Or stumble over that big rock
For then you'll downward sail

Musick Mountain

Sierra National Forest, Fresno County, California

Musick Mountain - 2011

Musick Mountain's calling you
As you walk up that trail
And as you progress step by step
Over hill and vale

Buck Rock

Sequoia National Forest, Tulare County, California

August 28, 1939: "With a blinding flash and a deafening roar, for a second time lightning struck the Buck Rock lookout house in the Sequoia National Forest but Don Ray, forest service lookout, escaped uninjured...sitting on his well-insulated stool, keeping track of the lightning strikes, was badly shaken but otherwise uninjured." *(Bakersfield Californian)*

Buck Rock 2011

Buck Rock's little house is so very nice
But it's so far to go
So many steps down and then back up
It doesn't pay to be slow

Beaver Ridge

Clearwater National Forest, Idaho County, Idaho

Beaver Ridge, August 17, 2011

August 15, 1919: "Wireless telephone reporting of a forest fire was invoked for what was said to be the first time in history today when lookouts in the Powell district, situated at Beaver Ridge notified the forest ranger at Lolo Hot Springs of a blaze at Beaver Ridge by means of this instrument." *(Nevada State Journal)*

The Beaver Ridge was far from home
But worthwhile just the same
The lookout wasn't open then
But I'm still glad we came

Jordan Peak

Sequoia National Forest, Tulare County, California

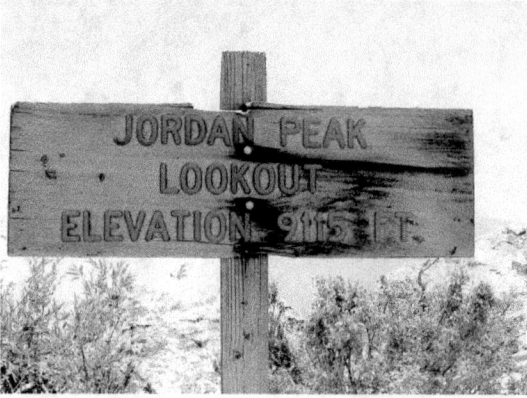

Jordan Peak, July 2011

August 23, 1923: "Edwin Laney, 86, from Pullman, Wash., set a hiking record when he negotiated the tramp from Camp Nelson, 35 miles east of here, to the top of Jordan Peak, a distance of 12 miles, in an altitude ranging from 4700 to 9000 feet. Ranger Young, stationed at Jordan Peak said that Laney was the oldest person to ever climb the peak." *(Oakland Tribune)*

Jordan Peak, California, 2011

Why was that ladder in the way
Of where I chose to sit?
I changed my mind and backed away
I did not like that pit

Stephenson Mountain
Ochoco National Forest, Oregon

Stephenson Point September 2009

July-August 1928: "A new fire finder has been installed in the tree at Stephenson Mountain where Lester Collins holds forth as lookout-fireman. It's a dandy, having a metal cover which resembles the lid of a garbage pail but eliminates the use of a canvas cover entirely. Let's have more of this type of fire finder. They are O.K." *(The Ochoconian)*

The new moon signifies a change
It's plain as it can be
To cast a light upon the plight
Of those who visit me

Rancheria Rock

Oregon Department of Forestry, Wheeler County, Oregon

Rancheria Rock September 4, 2009

July 1936: "Rancheria lookout station is located at the west end of the timber belt in Wheeler County, on the north side of the John Day River. The elevation of Rancheria is 4899 feet, which gives a very large view of the large area of timber land. There is a lookout cabin on the peak of a rock and on clear days we have a clear vision of all the snow peaks of the cascades and a large portion of the Blue Mountains south and east, including Rudio and Pisgah, another high point. The lookout has been maintained by the state during the fire season for the past eight years. A.P. Parrish." *(Umatilla Buckaroo)*

I am old and I am tired
My paint is wearing thin
My boards are cracking in the sun
It's sad the shape I'm in

Monument Mountain

Oregon Department of Forestry, Grant County, Oregon

Monument Mountain September 2009

August 10, 1951: "Aubrey Crum, at the lookout on Monument Mountain, has two unique pets. One is a lizard who makes his home in the woodpile. Whenever Crum picks up a piece of wood, the lizard is there to pick up bugs. The other pet, a porcupine, visits Crum each evening to get the table scraps." *(Blue Mountain Eagle)*

Once upon a hilltop rocky
Sat an outhouse with a view
But are those holes for looking out
Or someone looking in at you?

~

Those bloodshot eyes inside the door
Are watching as you sit
And read your book or contemplate
For just a little bit

Little Grayback

Oregon Department of Forestry, Josephine County, Oregon

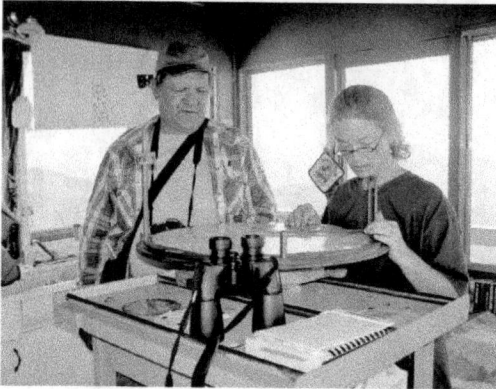

Ron Kemnow with lookout Sharon Prow 2011

1980: "Construction began on Little Grayback Lookout on July 1. Total completion is expected by the beginning of the 1981 season. It is located on Little Grayback Ridge which is about 8 miles east of Cave Junction.

Approximately 900 man hours were put into its construction thus far. Materials for the lookout were flown in by Forest Service helicopter. A lot of the materials were acquired from the old Waldo Mountain lookout. The new lookout provides better detection coverage than Waldo." *(Southwest Oregon District Annual Report, 1980)*

A few steps too far and you'll soar like an eagle
When seeking a place to park
You need a strong light for visits at night
Or just don't go out in the dark

I AM NEITHER HERE NOR THERE AND WOULD LIKE TO GO SOMEWHERE IN THE MIDDLE OF NOWHERE AND DO NOTHING ABOUT ANYTHING FOR A WHILE.....

Zenobia

Dinosaur National Monument, Moffat County, Colorado

Zenobia August 30, 2011

June 29, 1944: "Patrick Lopez is employed by the National Park Service in connection with the grazing service as a lookout at Zenobia Peak 50 miles northeast of Vernal, near Brown's Peak. Mr. Lopez's lookout station is equipped with a short wave radio set for contact with the grazing service. Mr. Lopez has an honorable army discharge and was employed at Bonanza prior to his new position." *(Vernal Express)*

The road was long, the road was tough
We almost didn't make it
There's the little house at last
Who'll be the first to take it?

~

A dinosaur itself it seems
It's been here long enough
It took almost a day to find
The road was very rough

High Park

Bighorn National Forest, Washakie County, Wyoming

High Park
August 23, 2012

A good place here to sit and rest
From climbing over rock
One obstacle was in our way
And that was the dad-burned lock!

Cougar Peak

Fremont National Forest, Lake County, Oregon

Cougar Peak, June 20, 2018

1911: In August, the Parker Hills fire was spotted in three places— Buck Mountain; Paisley by Jason Elder; and Cougar Peak by Lynn Cronemiller. *(Fremont History, Walt Dutton)*

1914: "As I recall, Bradley worked with us for a short period in grubbing willows from the station pasture and getting out material for the construction of a lookout tower on Cougar Peak." *(Fremont History, Walt Dutton)*

1914: "As to the tower on Cougar Peak, I remember getting out some pole material in 1913, 1914, or 1915 to be used in constructing a tower there. But the tower certainly was not up in 1914...I remember visiting the tower in later years when there was a tower directly over the rock monument." *(Letter from Walt Dutton to his brother Ed, January 20, 1963)*

Recalling all those thunder storms
I've survived many a blast
And now I sit here all forlorn
Thinking about the past

Dog Mountain

Fremont National Forest, Lake County, Oregon

Dog Mtn., Lake County
Oregon June-29, 2018

1918: The lookout duties were provided by Bertha Covert.

1926: A standard D-6 cupola lookout house was constructed. The lookout was equipped with a #4 Improved Osborne fire finder.

1947: A 14x14 Aladdin style lookout house with no catwalk was completed, having started the year before. The garage was moved from its former location, one quarter mile from the house. The cost of building this lookout was $2,700.

1997: A new lookout house was constructed.

Dog Mountain has a new outhouse
The old one sits in brush
'Tis better so if you need to go
And you are in a rush

Hickman Butte

Mt. Hood National Forest, Clackamas County, Oregon

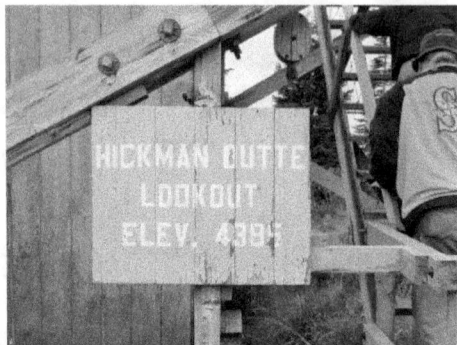

Hickman Butte September 17, 2011

September 17, 1928: "All the forest service lookouts are off duty for the season with the exception of the one on Hickman Butte, and he is building a new cabin to be ready for next summer." *(Morning Oregonian)*

July 14, 1955: "Jim Langdon reports that the road to Hickman lookout was opened last Friday...usually this road is free of snow by the 20th of June. This year the Forest Service plowed through snow drifts ten feet deep for a stretch of three miles. The same condition exists on Zig Zag Mt. Road." *(The Sandy Post)*

Hickman Butte seems lonely
But flowers line the walk
Tempting strollers on this path
To stop a while and talk

Snowboard Ridge

Oregon Department of Forestry, Wheeler County, Oregon

Snowboard - September 4, 2009

1935: A tower built of logs and lumber was constructed for a cost of $300.

August 1936: "Four years ago I went to work in the fire service... [in] a low swampy meadow in the forest. The mosquitoes were so bad they would puncture automobile tires. I rode three miles on horse back to a suitable point where I used a tree for a lookout. Today I am...in a modern tower with up-to-date equipment, a lovely garage, and a nice little house to live in. M.J. Campbell, guard." *(Umatilla Buckaroo)*

1962: Someone climbed to the catwalk and shot through the building shutters about center height of the windows, hitting the stove pipe and dampers on the way through.

Its roof is green, its door is down
It's Snowboard's little house
The little stepstool is for your feet
If you're scared by a little mouse

Kennaday Peak

Medicine Bow National Forest, Wyoming

Kennaday Peak Lookout, Wyoming August 20, 2012

Double duty this one does
On a green sky-high knob
Storage underneath the roof
And a seat for the lookout to do his "job"

Roman Nose Mountain
Siuslaw National Forest, Oregon

Carol VanCurler Photo

John Karnowsky Photo – 1960s

Photo by Ron Kemnow July 2008

His outhouse was open air
Should've been in a tent
For when lady hikers came along
Oh! What em-bar-rass-ment!

Black Mountain

Big Horn National Forest, Sheridan County, Wyoming

Black Mountain August 22, 2012

July 27, 1940: "Foreman Jack Young with 25 men and one leader is working on the Black Mountain Lookout. He has completed the interior carpenter work, staining, chinking, etc., and is building a rock walk or ramp up to the entrance of the building. It is expected that Lookout Shoemaker will move into the building this week although it will not be entirely completed until about August 7." *(CCC Camp F-3-W, Tongue River, inspection, October 3, 1940)*

What a classy little outhouse
Log cabin on a mountain high
It seems as though in this rarified air
You could reach out and touch the sky

Sheep Mountain

Big Horn National Forest, Johnson County, Wyoming

Sheep Mountain August 22, 2012

July 22, 1938: "Fred Foster, Forest Service lookout, was here Thursday for examination of an ear deafened Wednesday afternoon when lightning struck the lookout station on Sheep mountain, 32 miles west of Buffalo. Windows were shattered by the bolt, instruments were destroyed, telephone wiring was damaged and Foster's bed was set afire. The lookout repaired the telephone wiring and notified Forest Ranger U.J. Post. Forest Service officials said it is unusual for lightning to cause damage at lookout station, as all stations are wired as thoroughly as possible for fire protection. *(Billings Gazette)*

*This little round barrel
Had done its bit
Then 'twas filled with garbage
It's full of it*

Spruce Mountain

Medicine Bow National Forest, Albany County, Wyoming

Spruce Mountain August 28, 2011

A red stripe up the middle
Makes it a cheery place to sit
The orange splashboard does its part
To make it quite a hit

7-Mile Hill

Near Tok, Alaska

7 Mile Hill, near Tok, Alaska - Photos by Doug Fales 2016

Christy James, lookout on 7-Mile Hill during the summers of 2015 and 2016, and part of 2017, said, "That lookout spot is just a rock point on the edge of the ridge. I heard they were going to put a house of some kind up there."

When asked about her experiences as a lookout, she said, "The wind up on the hill gets pretty strong. In the hot summer, it sure feels good."

As to the question of whether she had spotted any fires, she replied, "Just fires in stove pipes. Nothing in the woods" and that sometimes someone is burning their lawn during a "burn suspension" or "burn ban."

She also said, "Lightning might chase you off the knob during a thunder storm," and that she has been chased off more than once... "Some people are scared of lightning. I usually let it get pretty close." *(From an interview with Christy James, July 13, 2018)*

Here's a place to watch for fires
And grouse and arctic hares
And ptarmigan and caribou
And maybe grizzly bears

Calimus Butte

Klamath Indian Agency>Oregon Department of Forestry>Winema National Forest, Oregon

Lookout Sharon Prow and Ron Kemnow July 10, 2018

July 20, 1920: "Wire whether you will come Klamath Indian Reservation. Work to build and guard cabin furnish your own tools and subsistence say six dollars a day. Christ Lund will assist you. West" *(Western Union telegram to J.C. Miller from Walter West, Superintendent Klamath Indian Agency)*

1930: The lookout on Calimus Butte [which was built in 1920], was torn down and replaced with a new cupola structure during July. *(FY Annual Report, Klamath Agency)*

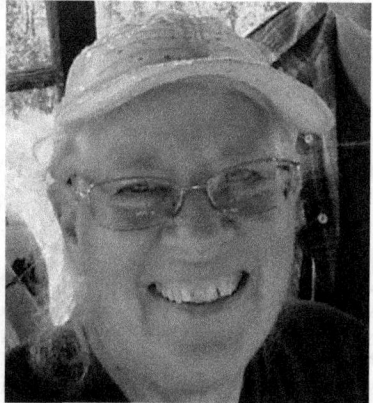

Lookout Jeannie
Petrinovich
Calimus Butte 2016
Photo by Jeannie

This outhouse looks too modern
The lookout's very old
Built in nineteen-thirty
At least that's what I'm told

Dutchman's Peak

Rogue River National Forest, Jackson County, Oregon

Dutchman's Peak, August 2007

This one's lying down to rest
It won't work any more
It's old and scarred and all beat up
It's just an old eyesore

McCart

Bitterroot National Forest, Ravalli County, Montana

McCart August 12, 2012

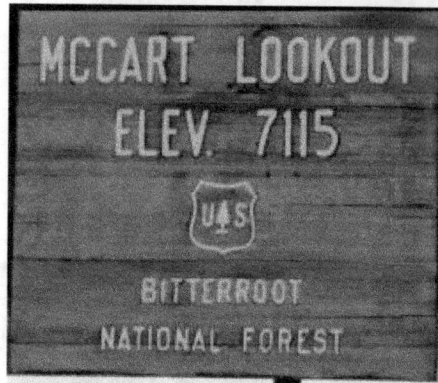

A round native timber tower with an L-4 observation cab was constructed in 1939.

It's hiding out there in the brush
The trees are closing in
So please don't go there in a rush
Use some discipline!

Hell's Half Acre Mountain

Bitterroot National Forest, Idaho County, Idaho

Hell's Half Acre - August 11, 2012

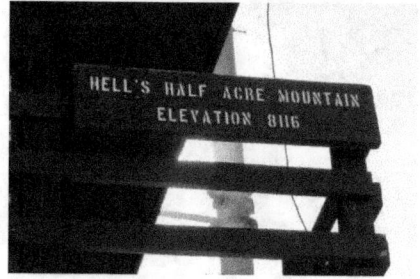

July 26, 2013: The lookout was wrapped in a fire retardant material as a precaution to an oncoming wildfire threat. The lookout staff were temporarily moved to Salmon Mountain. **September 3, 2017:** The lookout was wrapped and the staff evacuated by helicopter.

This poor sad relic's out of use
Old age has worn it down
An outhouse or a storage shed?
She's asking with a frown

Sheephorn Mountain

Salmon National Forest, Lemhi County, Idaho

Sheephorn
August 8,
2012

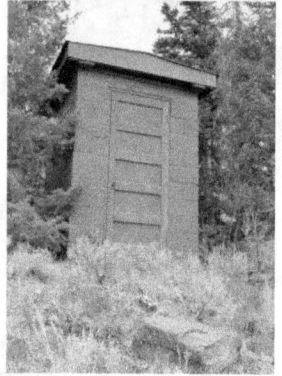

July 25, 1935: "Chancey Stroud was treated to a surprise last Thursday morning when on arising, he discovered, as he supposed, a tramp asleep on his living room couch. But when he sought to arouse the fellow to order him out he found it to be only Jimmy Waddington who had returned about midnight from the Hat creek fire, and too dirty and weary to go properly to bed had flung himself on the couch and was sleeping the sleep of utter exhaustion." *(Recorder Herald)*

The clouds are low and threatening
A chill is in the air
But here's a sight to cheer you up
In this cozy little lair

Stein Mountain

Salmon National Forest, Lemhi County, Idaho

Stein Mountain August 6, 2012

1925: "Lightning had struck Stein Mountain and his wife was badly burned...send a man with horses as he and his wife were starting down the mountain on foot. Mrs. Taylor was burned on the arms...the Taylors did not go back to a lookout again." *(From an interview with Ralph W. Dean by Thomas G. Alexander)*

September 2, 1953: "Lyman Dye was taken to his home at Idaho Falls to recover from a gunshot wound inflicted accidentally while shooting crows...the .22 caliber pistol discharged when Dye inadvertently dropped it while he was about to shoot a crow...the slug entered his right leg just above the knee..." *(The Recorder Herald)*

That little flap
Lets in the breeze
While the screen keeps out
The bugs 'n' bees

Swan Lake Mountain

Klamath Indian Agency>Oregon Department of Forestry>Winema National Forest, Klamath County, Oregon

Swan Lake Mountain July 15, 2018

An eighty foot steel tower was purchased in 1930 and erected in 1932. A ground cabin for living quarters was built in 1934. Construction of a truck trail to Swan Lake Point was started in 1937 but was delayed because of insufficient funds.

This pile of remains is all that's left
Of an outhouse that once stood proud
The lookout tower is long gone too
The footings lie under a shroud

Mule Peak

Sequoia National Park, Tulare County, California

Mule Peak, California July 2011

August 29, 1947: "Lookouts on Mule Peak and Tobias Peak, in the Sequoia National Forest, reported they sighted two California condors, now almost extinct, in the vicinity of Slate Mountain, east of Camp Nelson. They said the condors are male and female and are nesting on Slate Mountain." *(Fresno Bee)*

Sit here a while and watch the birds
Condors in the sky
They swoop and turn to watch for prey
As they go sailing by

Bear Butte

Klamath Forest Protective Association, Klamath County, Oregon

Red cinder pit below Bear Butte

Bear Butte, August 18, 2016

June 10, 1937: "The lookout at Bear Flat...sighted a fire...and extinguished it. *(The Evening Herald)*

August 7, 1947: "A fire burning on the Klamath Indian Reservation had covered about four acres of virgin timber in the Little Yamsay unit by noon today...

The Klamath Forest Protective Association got news of the fire from the lookout on Bear Butte at 10:12 a.m. Thursday and sent two men immediately to investigate. The blaze was too much for this limited crew and the Indian Service fire fighters were called to assist.

The Indian Service plane was circling the location, guiding volunteer assistants to the spot." *(Herald and News)*

1949: A lookout house was constructed at a cost of $177.83.

June 12, 1964: "The first lightning fire in the KFPA district this year broke out in a tree about six miles southeast of Bear Flat...The lightning strike set the tree afire despite...a large quantity of rain. A thin sliver of smoke from the tree was noted by the lookout station at Bear Flat...firefighters said they walked past the tree five or six times before it emitted a puff of smoke, betraying the fire." *(Herald and News)*

The cabin sits up on that knob
To climb it there's no rush
There is no little outhouse there
But there's a lot of brush

Horsefly Mountain

Fremont National Forest, Klamath County, Oregon

Horsefly August 25, 2016

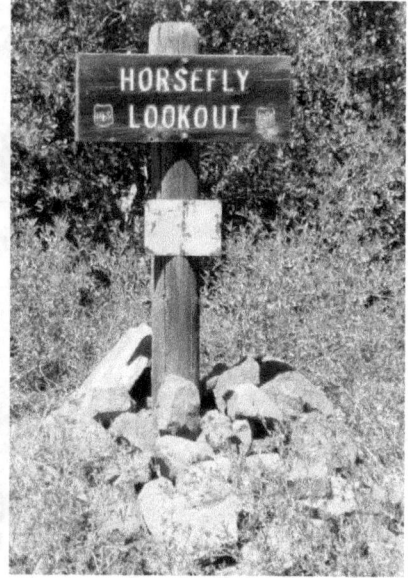

February 1, 1936: "At the time we started [construction of the telephone line] the ground was bare...but weather conditions have certainly changed. We are working in two feet of snow, and the work of setting a pole has practically doubled. In order that we may be able to do this at the present time it is necessary to clean all the snow away over a space of six to eight feet across, and then we are ready to dig the hole...stringing the wire, putting the insulators on etc., has all developed into quite a chore on account of the depth of the snow, but this article is not to wail and moan about deep snow, and unfavorable construction conditions, but is only put in to emphasize the fact that I never heard a member of my crew curse the weather or offer a word of complaint, no matter how tough the going has been." *(The Bly Snowdrift, CCC)*

The Buoys and Gulls roosting place
Or so it would appear
There's only room for one inside
Now do take turns, you hear?

Buoys
Gulls

Ingram Guard Station
Fremont National Forest, Lake County, Oregon

Ingram Guard Station August 30, 2016

This guard station is neat as a pin
With a log sauna by the creek
And you can see in the old outhouse
If you want to take a peek

~

For a place to rest this is the best
There is an old stump-chair
The buildings all are painted barn red
And a unique fence is there

Robinson Butte

Rogue River National Forest, Jackson County, Oregon

Robinson Butte
August 28, 2016

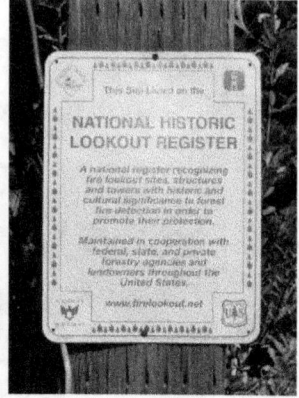

July 23, 1935: "During the height of the storm Sunday night Mrs. Herb Wright, wife of the lookout fireman stationed at Robinson Butte, was temporarily stunned by a bolt of lightning that struck a short distance from her. She was attending a forest service telephone while her husband was work on a nearby fire." *(Medford Mail Tribune)*

Robinson Butte has been condemned
There's a Historic Register plaque
The steps are gone, the outhouse is locked
We left and never went back

Sugarpine Mountain

Winema National Forest, Klamath County, Oregon

Sugarpine Mountain August 18, 2016

1970: The lookout tower and cab were airlifted from its original site at Fort Klamath.

*Sugarpine is a sweet sounding name
And a sweet little lookout too
With a comfort station that's one of the best
Just waiting for me or you*

Bald Butte

Fremont National Forest, Lake County, Oregon

2005 Ron Kemnow Photo

Bald Butte August 30, 2016

1911: The butte was used as a patrol lookout

October 2, 1931: "Just before reaching Ingram Station we turn off to Bald Butte. The Forest Service lookout towers are not built on hills convenient for automobiles and the climb takes about everything that the engine can give." *(Lake County Tribune)*

1964: The last year this lookout was staffed full time.

1994: In September the lookout renovation was completed. After two years of volunteer work, the Passport in Time project made the lookout house wheelchair accessible, but otherwise restored it to original specifications. A new toilet with an asphalt path topped off the project. Now the lookout is a very popular site in the recreational rental program.

They cleaned it out and fixed it up
To use it as a rental
But watch the weather while you're there
It can be temperamental

Deer Mountain

Bitterroot National Forest, Ravalli County, Montana

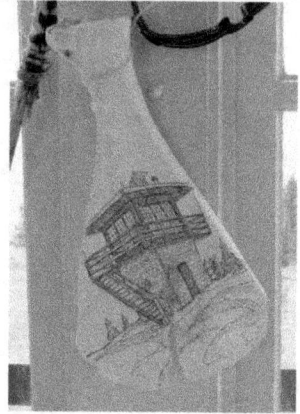

Deer Mountain
August 13, 2012

Deer Mountain's lookout was so creative
He did interesting art
But the lookout outhouse was very modest
It was a thing apart

Big Knob

Pulaski County, Kentucky

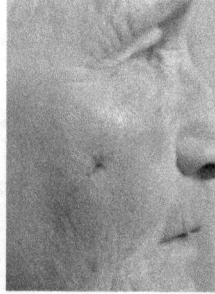

Big Knob, Kentucky May 28, 2018

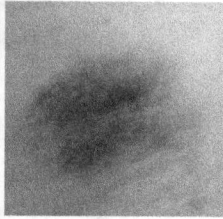

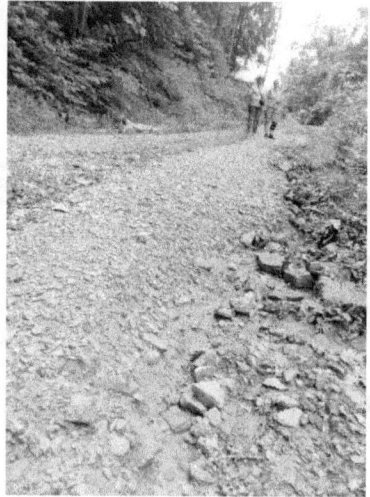

I saw a snake; I turned and fell
My face crashed on a rock
But I hiked on up to that lookout—
I may have been in shock

~

Unique design, a little squashed
I won't go over there
I've seen enough Kentucky snakes
(See how white it's turned my hair?)

Ulysses Mountain

Salmon National Forest, Lemhi County, Idaho

August 6, 2012

1924: A Salmon Forest lookout report shows no improvements at this site. The lookout climbed trees to view the surrounding country.

September 20, 1951: "The Forest proposes to sell, donate, abandon or destroy on or after October 22. 1951, the following property found to be unservicable for government use: 7 mile telephone line, No. 9 iron wire, grounded circuit, beginning at Ulysses Tower, approximately 5 miles North East of Indianola Ranger Station and continuing North for 7 miles to Indian Peak Lookout." *(The Recorder Herald)*

This poor old place was once so nice
Now rodents have moved in
The old outhouse is falling down
Just like an old tenpin

Near Zenobia

Deer... oh dear! Zenobia deer!
I didn't mean to peek
When you needed a private moment
I should have turned my cheek

On the trail to Kerby Lookout

Do humans build a house for bears?
Equip it with a rail?
No! The bear just ambles on
And leaves it on the trail

~

A bear was there! He walked this trail.
He left his calling card
For little shacks he has no use
He leaves it in the yard